FIELD TRIPS
on the
RAPID TRANSIT

OTHER BOOKS

POETRY:
Selected Poems (1983)
The Clouds of That Country (1982)
Toward the Liberation of the Left Hand (1977)
The Dust Dancers (1977)
City Joys (1975)
The Invention of New Jersey (1969)
The Hurricane Lamp (1969)
PROSE:
Choreography Observed (1987)
The American Dance Festival (1987)
Ballet and Modern Dance: A Concise History (1986)
The One and Only: The Ballet Russe de Monte Carlo (1981)
The Nutcracker Ballet (1979)
Dance (1974)

FIELD TRIPS
on the
RAPID TRANSIT

Jack Anderson

Hanging Loose Press

Published by Hanging Loose Press
231 Wyckoff Street
Brooklyn, New York, NY 11217

The publisher wishes to thank the Literature Program of the New York
State Council on the Arts for support of the publication of this book.

These poems first appeared in the following publications: *Alcatraz, Another
Chicago Magazine, Beloit Poetry Journal, Caliban, Chelsea, Chiaroscuro, Confronta-
tion, Dirty Bum, Epiphanies, Exquisite Corpse, Giants Play Well in the Drizzle, Hang-
ing Loose, Hubbub, Images, Kayak, The Little Magazine, Oyez Review, Poetry East,
The Spirit That Moves Us, Tellus, Virginia Quarterly Review*

Cover painting by Louise Hamlin.

Cover design by Alice Soloway Design.

Library of Congress Cataloging-in-Publication Data

Anderson, Jack
    Field trips on the rapid transit / Jack Anderson.
       p.   cm.
    ISBN 0-914610-69-4 :   ISBN 0-914610-68-6 (pbk.) :
    PS3551.N366F54   1990
811'.54 — dc20   89-26913
                                         CIP

Produced at The Print Center., Inc., 225 Varick St.,
New York, NY 10014, a non-profit facility for literary
and arts-related publications. (212) 206-8465

CONTENTS

At Memphis Station

INSTRUCTIONS FOR VISITING
A STRANGE CITY

Observe its churches, theatres, and banks,
Its department stores and bus depot. If
One remains, stroll through its railroad station.
See whose statues stand in parks. Search out both
Grand hotels and corner bars near army
And navy stores. Look close. And then you'll know
What gods are honored here.

Open the Yellow Pages: scan the ads
For Dancing Schools and Restaurants, and note
Their names, the layouts for their ads, the line
Drawings in those ads. Now watch late movies
On TV and study the commercials
For local business firms. So shall you learn
What graces grace this place.

EXPERIENCES OF TRAVEL

In each stop on your itinerary, all the scenic, cultural, and historical attractions are closed on Sundays. Even the ruins have been packed away.

The same thing is true on Mondays.

And on Tuesdays. Wednesdays. Thursdays. Fridays.

And on Saturdays, as well.

*

After you tip him lavishly, the guard yawns, stirs, grumbles, takes a set of keys, opens a small heavy locked gate, and shows you something absolutely disgusting.

*

Carrying a beach umbrella, towels, suntan lotion, and a picnic basket, you start trudging from your hotel toward the ocean.

But the tide is ebbing and no matter how far from the hotel you get, the water still remains in the distance. Then it is night. And the waves roll in around you.

*

Exhausted from a hot day of travel, you rush into your hotel room and head straight toward the sink.

There, shining like a beacon on its shelf, is the water glass. You fill it from the tap and gulp down glass after glass of beautiful cold water.

The next morning, while packing, you spy a tiny sign at the back of a closet.

"Official notice," it says. "The water here is not safe to drink."

*

You fall desperately ill and try to ask the hotelkeeper for a doctor. But though you gesticulate, miming pain, he doesn't understand.

"A doctor," you say. "I want a doctor. A doctor."

At last, the light of comprehension dawns. "You want a doctor," he says. "I'll send for one now." And he dials a number and mutters something.

An hour later, an eminent philologist knocks on your door.

*

You go for a meal in a restaurant.

Just when you expect your soup to arrive, the entire restaurant staff walks out. Waiters, busboys, cooks, and kitchen helpers march from the restaurant into a house across the street.

You are left abandoned, hungry and alone, with no one to serve you and nothing to eat.

Yet from across the street come the most delicious odors of cooking imaginable.

*

The day you depart, the hotelkeeper returns your passport.

But, examining it, you discover that the photograph on it is not your photograph, the name beside the photograph is not your name, and the signature underneath is not your signature.

When you point this out to him, the hotelkeeper studies the passport and says, "Sir, as passport photographs go, that's a pretty fair likeness. And, see, there is your signature right here on the register."

But you can find no name or handwriting you recognize.

Later, back home, your friends stare at you perplexed. They wrinkle their brows and ask, "What have you done with yourself? Have you cut your hair? Let it grow long? Grown a moustache? Shaved off your beard? You look thinner. Fatter. Never better. Are you sure you're all right?"

DISCOVERY OF A HEAD

It seems there's this head in the oven.
Not my head.
Not any head I know.
It must be a head the last tenants left.

We'll just have to make the best of it, then,
Work around it.
We can slide the roast in on one side
And let the head stay where it is.
No problem.

It will be cozy there in winter.
In summer
We often eat salads,
So we won't disturb it much.
And if we do, well,
We all suffer from the heat sometimes.
That's life.

THE CAVES

Beneath these rolling fields
or hidden behind these rocks,
somewhere where no one can find them without effort,
somewhere you might not expect them to be,
they are:

worlds within this world,
worlds you pass by
or step over,
dark worlds, silent,

yet worlds with their own forests and plains,
worlds with mountains, canyons, cliffs,
and cities: there are cities here,
and streets,
streets lined with spires and blocks of towers,

and here are gardens, mazes, ruins
all made by no hands
from drops of water
no eye has seen,

and when you come upon this,
if ever you do,
you bring light to it then,

you behold it and, marveling,
let your sight define it:
this form without design,
this endless creation
perfect and purposeless.

AT MEMPHIS STATION

This is a poem you probably do not know.
I, too, do not know it.
I didn't write it, I've never read it.
It is someone else's poem,
a poem I've only heard about
that was written years ago
in a foreign language
by a traveler crossing this country by train.

Friends in that poet's country
who have mentioned it to me
call it a poem about waiting,
and from the way they describe it
it goes something like this:

At Memphis Station

It has been raining all day.
The train has scarcely moved.
And now it is stalled at Memphis station.

Word comes from the stationmaster:
the river is rising,
farms are in danger.
The train stays where it is, stalled
at Memphis station.

There is nothing to do.
You can stare out the window,
you can pace up and down
or step from the train
and pace on the platform.

The rain keeps falling.
Steam fogs the station.
There is nothing to do
but pace up and down.

Then a train pulls in
out of the fog
on the opposite track.
Men rush to the cars
and bear from the cars
the bodies of farmers,
their wives, and their children
drowned in the floods.

They set them on the platform
side by side in the rain.

(It rains and, oh,
I wish I could be
by the palm trees out West,
or if I can't be out West,
I wish I had taken
some other train to Memphis
to come here to Memphis
a week from today
or last week or yesterday
or any day but today
so I could stroll up and down
the nice streets of Memphis,
smoking my pipe
on the best streets of Memphis
where I might meet a Memphis girl
and stay with my girl and my pipe in a house
in some other part of Memphis
and I wouldn't have to be here
at Memphis station
seeing the bodies
brought to the platform,
oh I wish I had left, Lord,
before I saw this, oh Lord,
I wish I were anywhere
but Memphis station.)

But now the train pulls out
out of Memphis station;
picking up speed, it speeds through the rain,
the rest of the country lying before it.

Everything goes: station, floods, fog,
the drowned on the platform,
the traveler on the train....

*

The poem ends here
with everything gone.

And Memphis station,
which I've never seen,
I know only from this
poem I've never read:
this is not my poem,
At Memphis Station.

Yet the poem does exist:
It is someone's poem
in a foreign tongue.
It is something out there
I take on trust
like Memphis or you.

THE TOLEDO MUSEUM

One day, I knew I had had enough: I
couldn't take it any more. Yet I kept
my mouth shut.
                I just decided to go
where no one would dream of looking for me.
Then I thought: Toledo, Ohio, why
not? That's where I'd go—where I'd never been,
where I knew no one—I'd go there and hide
in the Toledo Museum of Art.

So I studied the atlas and said, "Yes,
this is it"
            —and came out of the tunnel:
I was in New Jersey. I bade farewell
to the New York skyline, and the freeway
carried me along high into the hills
of Pennsylvania, bare but for patches
of snow gone gray. I rounded curves with joy,
admired the rivers, and stopped to get gas
where pumps shone like beacons in morning fog.
I lived on coffee and donuts I bought
at the turnpike sweet shops.
                        Foundries loomed up,
coal mines, smelters, and steel mills, the smoke stacks
and furnaces of Pittsburgh at sunset.
I pulled into a motel with thick rugs,
wide beds, and passing trucks sang me to sleep.

The new day brought Ohio, Lake Erie
on my right, still frozen over, the wind
blowing, ice cracking and thundering. This
was Ohio all day. Farms came and went
and tumults of signs clamoring "Cleveland,"
but I kept on, headed for Toledo.

And one day I was there—in Toledo
where I wanted to be, where I would hide.
I went to the Toledo Museum
and hid where I'd planned.
                I'm still there, somewhere.

No one has found me, no one has bothered
to search so far for me. Most people don't
even realize I'm gone: they may think
they still see me as ever, but they don't
see me, it must be someone else, for one
day I decided I'd had enough and
I opened the atlas to a city
where I knew no one and no one knew me,
but where I knew there was this museum,
and I said goodbye and hid myself deep
in the Toledo Museum of Art.

LATE MUSIC

In the pleasure of a piano sonata
And black coffee at midnight,
I can taste the music:
Bitter, warm, alive, and rattling,
It keeps me awake, awake in the real.

*

An order goes out to everything:
Things set forth on a journey.

I, too, shall be gone:
Transported, yet present
Still drinking black coffee
On the heights above sleep.

*

All things return to the first thought of them.
Then all things come back to us better, yet the same.
Yet nothing shall ever be the same again.

I can scarcely remember
Who I've been,
Or when.
And yet whatever is, is here.

ABSENCE

Not abandonment . Nor severing .
Absence . Your absence . Your being gone
Those times you are not with me . How rooms
Widen . How their objects stand out to

Proclaim their own shape . Alone . I walk
Among them, touch little, say less . I
Sleep by myself, see sun in the panes
And night there . I study in those panes

My reflections . There is nothing else .
I take in your absence . I haunt it .
It belongs to me and to these rooms

Until you return . Then we shall give
Back your going and claim this space ours
To be in as we are . We are here .

Field Trips
on the
Rapid Transit

AROUND HERE

the hardware store
became a grocery

the Puerto Rican grocery
turned Korean
with a special health food section
just about when the Italian fruit stand
also went Korean

a pizzeria
is where the doctor's office was
the doctor moved around the corner

a men's social club
became a dress shop
another men's club
went into the smaller place across the street / it's still there
where the travel agent was

nothing's ever worked here
an Italian restaurant
a pastry cafe
a steakhouse with jazz piano
a breakfast brunch and luncheon spot with a long list of omelets
obviously people keep thinking there ought to be food here
but nothing works
it's empty again / and again
there's someone fixing it up

where the greeting cards were
they're selling toys
where years before they sold antiques

I've never been sure just what this fancy store
actually sells

where the Chinese laundry was
is covered with scaffolding
but the laundryman has opened
a new laundry by the church

in the next apartment
when I moved in
there lived this young couple
two schoolteachers
then came the bartender
then the playwright
now there's this insomniac
who plays the radio late

across the hall lived an old man
who coughed a lot
time passed
and the door was open and I saw painters inside
and he was gone and never came back
there's a fat woman there now
she seldom goes out

the woman upstairs
used to walk a dog
a little yapper named Velvet
after a while it got deaf
but it didn't stop yapping
one day I saw the woman
without her dog
so I asked her "How's Velvet?"
she looked at me strangely
"Velvet's been dead for almost a year"

I can't remember
what was here before the shoe store
but something was
and I saw it

TRANSCONTINENTAL

After the directional arrow pointing out the exit lane and the descent on the freeway ramp and the slow journey from stop light to stop light along the dusty boulevard with its drive-ins and filling stations and the turn onto the residential street where the greenery increases as the road climbs the hill, there on the crest of the hill is your house looking down from its cliff upon the whole city spread in the sunlight below, and there you are now, climbing out of the swimming pool, drops of water clinging to your tanned skin as you cross the patio to a deck chair with a towel on it and, after drying yourself off, you slip into a pair of sandals and sit at a table guarded by a sun-shade and, still wearing your damp bathing suit, you start typing on a portable, the steady clatter of keys drifting across the neighbors' lawns and into the valley as you describe how the snow is falling outside my window, sticking to the branches of trees and to the pickets on the fence in back, and how, wearing torn jeans and an old flannel shirt with the sleeves rolled up, I sit at my desk in the gray afternoon, the radiator hissing faintly, the light of a single lamp falling over my left shoulder upon the sheet of notebook paper on which I am writing with a stubby pencil about how after the freeway exit gives way to the ramp and the slow journey past drive-ins in the sun-glare and the turn up the shady side street to where your house is, you swim, a blurry shape moving underwater, then climb the ladder at the far end of the pool, pausing for a moment in the late morning light to shake the water off your tanned back before you cross the patio and sit at your typewriter as both of us realize that soon we must give each other a face and a voice and words to say.

THE ISLAND

On the Upper West Side
Broadway widens
into something like a boulevard
with a strip of greenery down the center
and at each cross-street between the uptown and downtown lanes
a little island with a park bench

where you can sit
amidst traffic,
the uptown traffic surging toward you, then swerving off,
the downtown traffic escaping the other way,

you can just sit and let this happen
and drink a coffee-to-go from the deli
or you can eat a cheese Danish
or spoon yogurt and think

of comets streaking the night sky of stones,
of telephones ringing in the bellies of whales,
of mirrors breaking into the secret codes of icebergs,
of sphinxes toppling pyramids with the silence of their roars.

and while you think this you can watch the traffic,
the cars, buses, taxis,
the trucks, the bikes and motorbikes
and sometimes a horsedrawn cab from Central Park,
and people will always be pasing,
they'll come to your island, pause for the light,
then go on
and be followed
by more people at the next light:

strollers, shoppers, dog walkers,
pokers in trash cans, old ladies with canes,
babies in prams,
office workers with briefcases or little brown lunch bags,
drinkers sipping something suspicious from their own brown bags,
ballet students with dance bags

—so many kinds of bags:
handbags, shoulder bags, book bags, record bags—

and you'll be able to keep an eye out for
hats, ties, collars,
buckles, belts, boots,
umbrellas, sweaters, rings, earrings, bracelets, eyeglasses,
creases in pants, baggy pants, tight pants, scuff marks on shoes,

and all this will be going on as you sit
and you can sit there such a long time people could think you owned
    the place

and cars may stop so motorists can ask
how to get to the Holland Tunnel or St. Patrick's Cathedral
and you'll know, you can tell them,

and you'll feel like a monarch there on your island
and you may even try stretching out an arm as if to make the traffic
    stop on this side and *go* away that way
until you find yourself waving things forward and holding them back
    like a conductor at Lincoln Center
and people will give you strange looks but pass politely on
and you'll just smile beatifically and raise your arms to the heavens
where clouds are flying like flags across the sun
and on each is written JOY
in big neon letters in invisible ink.

PART OF A DAY

There are times when streets
fill with the smells
of coffee,
spices,
or baking bread,

times when it seems
there is plenty for all,

and there are times filled
with soap smells
or disinfectant
when whole avenues come clean.

*

I learn

a friend has died,
killed himself.

Friends hadn't seen him for days,
so they broke open his flat
and found him.

He'd been borrowing money
and he had no money,
so he borrowed more money.

After a time,
he knew this mess
would only get worse.

Then he saved up pills.
He could think of nothing else.

*

Waiting for the subway,
I glanced toward the track
and there, limping along,
was a small dirty

black-and-white cat
and, behind it, the light
of an oncoming train.

I turned aside,
too late
to do anything.

(How did that cat
get there to start with?
How do you get
into such a spot?

And yet,
if the cat were small and smart enough
to hunch itself down
the train might have passed

over it:
it could have survived,
under certain conditions.

Still,
how long could it have stayed there
without getting hurt?

What could it have done to get out?)

*

It rained hard,
now it's bright,
but with a nip in the air:
November.

I wander through the streets,
taking things in,
reasonably content, yet...

*

I wish I knew what words could help.

THE REAL WORLD

He bought a motorcycle
And put his life in order:
Days, he worked in an office,
He wore a tie; nights, he wore

Black leather, and he and these
Other guys would ride around
On their bikes, and on weekends
There'd be club runs, wild parties,

Wild times until Monday rolled
Around again. He had it
All balanced: the day and night
Of him, his light and dark, his

Work, play, and passion. Then, one
Day, he started feeling odd,
Really out of it, and he
Came down with a strange disease

No one could explain or cure.
Now, not knowing how much time
Is left him, he sits for hours
In his room wondering, "Why?"

And whenever friends come by
To visit, they look at him
And wonder, "Why?" And after
They leave they also ask, "Why?

"Why, stranger, are you writing
Everything down in this way,
Arranging his story in-
To four-line stanzas? What, pray,

"Can you possibly think you're do-
Ing by taking such pains
To make sure each line contains
Seven syllables, not

"Six or eight? What, by all this,
Can you hope to add here?
What do you wish to keep away?
What are you trying to do?
What are you trying to say?"

POEM FOR A BIRTHDAY

I have more and more years, less
and less time: what have I gained?
What has anyone my age
gained? We stay poor in a poor
world that no one can live in.
When has anyone ever
really lived in this world? How
has it been possible? When?
How many years must it be
—and how many wars—since I
first feared war? Yet now there is
new talk of war, the same war
as ever, and still we fear
new panic and pestilence,
riot and pillage, just as
of old: we are still that poor,
so how can anyone live
here where we are? Who can say,
"I have lived my life fully;
I have had a rich life"—who
has been given such spaces
of time with such luxuries
of days to hoard or squander
at will? I used to think this
would come, our rewards would come,
but new years came with new wars,
new sores and plagues, new shouters
with stones, new smiters with swords,
and they were always the same
ones, struggling as hard as we
did, with no more time than we
had, demanding our strength, our
time, and they kept returning,
doing what they felt had to
be done, so we spent our time
—we spent ourselves—on them, they
claimed us, they took up our time;
and now we have less time, and
there is always no time left

to live in the world. Who has
lived in the world ever? What
fool, villain, liar dare boast,
"Look, I have lived in the world;
see, I have lived out my life?"

CITY BREAKFAST

There is almost no such thing
as a really bad breakfast place:

come early, if there's a window
sit by it, see

how they rush in
for their juice, eggs, and *Daily News*,

then they're out
and others come

while the radio plays
traffic reports and weather

and commercials for a bank,
and maybe a waitress drops a plate,

the whole place
crashing along,

yet some just stay:
that bunch in the back booth

smoking, laughing,
kidding the waitress, shooting the breeze,

with time on their hands
they're making the most of it

until they, too, have
to get up and go, now

the joint thins out,
you're all that's left

—you and that guy in need of a shave,
you and that lady crumbing a muffin—

ordering refills on coffee,
watching the trucks pass:

the morning has begun,
it's all around you

and you get to be
your part of it

when you feel it's time
to leave a tip and leave

—so you do.

THIS PARK, THIS SUMMER HOUR

They're men from offices
sitting in the sun,
collars open,
on little benches under trees.
They take off their jackets,
loosen their ties more,
they're almost in old clothes
they wouldn't dare wear in the office.
They look at nothing and yawn
or smoke, read,
doze.

*

There is a fountain playing
where the paths meet,
there is a fountain
that goes on and on,
water streaming around its figures —
it draws the park toward it,

and there is a fountain playing
around us:

the street,
its trucks and cars
going on and on through the crossings,

it has no need of us,
we make none of it happen,

yet it draws us in,
holds us in its playing,
figures of a fountain.

*

The sun is warm,

*but it could be midwinter
far away under stars
on a plain in the snow*

where an old woman calls:
"Boris," she says,
"have you fed the wolves,
have you watered the bears?"

A page turns, eyes blink

and another story
starts to tell.

                  *

I could smile
at all these men
doing only this now,

now they are good folk,
they will not hurt.

A WALK THROUGH
THE HISTORIC DISTRICT

There are statues here
— half-forgotten leaders,
all-but-forgotten preachers —

that loom from the shadows
when you least expect it,
lifting an arm to heaven
or pointing a finger straight at you,
gaze lowered upon the bloodied earth
or head thrown back to defy the storm
or fixing you in the eye
and not letting you out of their sight:

they confront you,
they are smug,
they are dead,
they can afford to be smug,
having acted as they did

they have the right
to call you into action,
they tell you you must choose,
you have no choice,
you must face your destiny,
mend your ways,
take up the banner
and march to glory
so you can be remembered
and be smug and stand forever,
arms raised in exhortation
or pointed in accusation

forcing anyone who passes
to stop and think,
"Whoever they were,
those statues in the dusk,
they were better souls than we are,"
before moving on with new resolve.

FIELD TRIPS ON THE RAPID TRANSIT

1

SMITH-9TH ST.
highest station on the el
the trains rise up from the subway here

    their metal at one
        with water and air

The tracks curve as they approach
      and riding the sweep of them
           is like riding the Sound on the first warm day
               no matter what day of the year it may be

And then the station   tracks caught
      between walls:
         a canyon
         with its rapids

Watching
from the street
      you behold the light industry
           of cars ascending
           into the bright blue sky
and you see come down
      great thunders of cars:
           machines in their elements
           storming away.

2

There is an old elevated line in Brooklyn where trains no
longer run. Yet the structure remains, rusting, with tracks
ripped up and ties gone. Still, there it is, what's left of it.

You can follow it, if you like, though it goes past nothing
much in particular: nondescript streets with small houses
and apartments, the sort of houses that have statues of Mary
out front. Next come a playground, some garages, warehouses,
loading docks.

From time to time, there's a station. But the stairs to
the platforms are boarded over. And the station windows are
broken, of course. Sometimes whole sections of walls may be
gone.

People dump stuff along here, things as irrelevant as the
line itself: leaky sofa cushions, flat tires, dented cans,
smashed mirrors and beer bottles, raggedy clothing, one
scuffed boot (but never its mate). You know what I mean:
worn things, battered things, things no one needs.

It goes on like this, this line does, as obvious and useless
as an old woman's sigh over days gone by. But when it reaches
the graveyard at Fort Hamilton Parkway it dips and vanishes
into the ground. And then

> you sometimes
> imagine
>
> the last train
> still moving
>
> through the graves
> below you
>
> like a fish
> in a gulf
>
> no sounding
> can fathom.

3

A slowing in the tunnel,
then up to the surface,
the shedlike station,
the tracks in a trench
open to the sky.
The sign reads PROSPECT PARK
and I start to remember
                    (but at first I can't)
something else, some-

thing more,

        more important

about this place

    (*Mal*-something)

             (yes)

something worse

        Mal-   (evil, bad, sick) (yes)

        Mal-

MALBONE STREET

Yes, this is Malbone Street Station, November 1, 1918:

Only a small yellow light shone on the notice giving the
    authorized speed for the curve in the tunnel: 6 miles
    an hour.
When the train with the inexperienced motorman passed the
    light, it was doing 45.
The front wheels of the first car swung around the curve.
    Standing passengers lost their grip on the straps and
    fell to the floor.
Now aware of the danger, the motorman tried to brake. But
    the wheels of the first car had already left the track.
The first car was hurled against the tunnel ceiling. Wood
    and glass impaled the passengers. The third car crashed
    into the second, the fourth car into the third. The fifth
    was unharmed. There were dead and dying everywhere.
And when some of the survivors staggered from the cars, they
    brushed up against the third rail and were instantly electro-
    cuted.
97 dead, 200 injured
at Malbone Street, at Malbone Street.

             *

No station now bears the name MALBONE STREET:
it was a name too terrible to keep.

This station is PROSPECT PARK.

Trees rise up at the top of the trench,
vines creep down along the trench walls,
you could guess you're near a park, but

43

what happened close by once is almost forgotten,
the weeds have grown over it,
therefore nothing has happened here,
so far as anyone can tell,
it is the same today as it ever was,
on schedule, without incident:

> this is Prospect Park
> where people walk
> on Sundays when it's sunny.

4.

You have come so far you can imagine nothing further.
But here is where you can change to go still further one.

A whole tree of stations grows from the subway here
Affording shelter and shade like any tree on a hill.

Deep in the roots of BROADWAY-EAST NEW YORK station
You feel slow as a worm, you can't seem to get moving.

The platform looks longer than the ride to Far Rockaway.
But then there are steps and a pale light — and it's daylight.

Escalators ascend the trunk of this tree
And you're already above the trees outside.

You're up at the top where the el lines branch
Above you, below you, on all sides with their tracks:

Platforms over platforms, stations over stations
Shaking in the wind as the trains pass like seasons,

And tracks reaching upward, tracks twisting down around,
But always branching, branching out from this place, and

Everything moving now, moving to a different place,
Yet everything joined, a part of one system,

As you, too, are part of it as you make your connection
And continue onward to the end of this line.

The Guided Tour

THE GREAT DAYS OF BALLOONING

I was walking kicking stones down a country lane
And a balloon sailed over me
I was sitting fishing one noon on the dock
And a balloon sailed over me
I was conning my Latin grammar in the park
And along came a balloon

And the balloon sailed over
The farmers' fields
The cows in the fields
The horses and farmers plowing in the fields
A stream with its fish
And old mills waterwheels scarecrows and hedgerows

And I could imagine acrobats dangling from balloons
And trained apes swinging from trapezes on balloons
And a balloon so big it could hoist up an elephant
And a balloon so light it could fly to the moon
And a balloon making music with Aeolian harps and windchimes
And a balloon borne like a chalice by the heavenly host

I was bowing to bid my neighbor-lady good-morrow
When a balloon sailed over me
I was saying my prayers at a wayside shrine
When a balloon sailed over me
I was setting out on the highroad to seek my fortune
When a balloon came past

And the balloon flew over
My house my neighbor's house the mayor's house the manorhouse
The garden house like a temple the garden arch like a ruin
The square with its fountain alehouse and market stalls
The Castle the Cathedral the Palace of Justice
The ships on the sea the troops on maneuvers

And I could imagine balloons rescuing lost hikers in the hills
And post-balloons delivering letters by dropping them at Town Halls
And omnibus-balloons taking visitors to the sights
And hospital-balloons for coughers in need of fresh air
And balloons equipped with spyglasses to spy down on robbers
And balloons with soldiers patrolling the skies

I was going my way and a balloon sailed over me
And a man in the balloon waved a big plumed hat
And another man in the balloon held a dog in his arms
And a goat stood beside him and someone my age with a pussycat
And I called up, envious, "Where are you going, my friends?"
And though I couldn't hear their answer they seemed to be laughing

And I thought to myself, "Lord, what an adventure!"

LIFE ON THE MOON

Like anyplace else, it has its problems. It also has its advantages, especially when it's waxing. Then we step forth from our huddle, happy to find one more inch of ground to hold us. And the ground continues to spread on all sides until it stretches as far as we can see. Men and women stride this way and that and never bump into anyone. Children gambol on the leas. Rabbits bound across the moors. Sometimes we dance for hours on end—that is, until someone feels the ground slip out from under his feet and someone else hears a faint rustle of pebbles that gradually becomes a rattle of stones. We know this can mean only one thing: the waning has begun. It continues. The ground shrinks. It trembles. Canyons open, gorges yawn, avalanches bear whole cliffs away. One must be careful where one steps, for where the ground does not crumble it turns ominously spongy. In time, one grows adept at hopping from stone to stone for safety. But newcomers here—and even some of our very own elderly—often prove not quite quick enough. So they vanish forever into outer space. At last, there is almost no ground left. We're joined together in a huddle once more and, still, some people can't find a toehold. They, too, float off from us. At last comes the moment even oldtimers dread: the moment we feel nothing at all beneath our feet. It's only for an instant, yet it's real. Now nothing exists but terror and the void, for no matter how often we've lived through this, we still fear we are doomed. Yet we also try to summon up faith and to reason out that all is not lost. And we are right: a sliver of ground firms to support our feet—only a sliver, yet it is there. We are saved again, safe on the solid ground of a newborn moon.

THE GUIDED TOUR

Over there is a rock
Shaped like a rock,
And next to it is a rock
Shaped like a stone.

But over here is a rock
That isn't a rock,
We just call it a rock.

And here is where a rock used to be.

Fancy that and hurry along:
You are getting too close for comfort.

Birds would roost here
If birds ever roosted here,
But because of wolves
Birds don't ever roost here:
You see, there are no wolves here,
Not even in song and story.

Behind that tree there lives a mitten
Lost by Mindy Hicks at the age of eight.

When people reach this spot
They usually pant from the effort.
Can you guess how many pantings
Have been panted on this spot?
And how far they would reach
If they were stacked in a pile?

And this place is best defined
As a cave above ground.

If this were a cliff
With water going over it,
It would be a waterfall,
And if all its water were laid out flat
And turned into sand,
It would be a desert.

So much for this place.

In this next place we think
The air is upside down.

You may pause for a blurred photograph
Or you may buy in our shop
Thousands of photographs
Of everything you've missed.

SLUMMING

Sometimes, Saturday nights,
before they went out
mother and father
used to laugh and say,
"Let's go slumming tonight."

I wonder what they meant.
I wonder where they went.

*

The few times I've been near,
the few times I've thought of it,
I've wondered about the Hide-A-Way,
that dump by the river.
What's there. I imagine

smoke,
dry coughs,
skinny arms, arms bloated with fat,
faces with too much makeup on,
jowls, brags, a pounding fist,
a bartender cooling it.

I wonder who goes there,
where they come from.

*

Just to find out,
maybe I should try it some night,
look it over, nurse a drink,
sit for hours on a barstool
watching the lights in the beer signs,
trying to keep out of trouble.

Then I would know,
then I could go
back.

But everyone else
would have to stay,
for everyone else there
never goes anywhere.

And I'll never go there, either.
I know.

                    *

I remember how mother and father
might say on a Saturday,
"Let's go slumming tonight,"
and make it their joke.

Yet they'd go somewhere.
I wonder where:
to a bar with a polka band, perhaps;
to a bar with a blues singer, maybe.
To that bar by the river, the Hide-A-Way?
Oh, never.
No one goes there.

RETIREMENT

For the longest time
they didn't quite know what to do with their time
until they discovered they liked to make every day
a Sunday drive for a Sunday dinner.
They'd worked hard all their lives for this, they thought,
they'd gone through so much—so why not?

They'd take off in their car
scouting out restaurants
with names like the Bobolink,
the Hideaway, the Homestead,
the Jolly Fishermen, the Fox and Hounds.
They got to know
almost every nice restaurant around;
they seemed to know
every good place in their part of the state.
And it wasn't just restaurants:
they learned about church suppers, Kiwanis Club cookouts,
and Legion Post fish fries.
They knew where to eat everywhere.

They'd put the question over breakfast:
"Where shall it be tonight?"
and spend the rest of the morning and all afternoon
making a list.
"Shall we stay here in town or go out in the country?
Is this a good night for the Swiss Chalet?
Or why not try
the Nahomac Gardens on Lake Nahomac
or the Golden Lion up in the hills?
And when's First Methodist's pancake feast?"

They'd drive into the night
in summer with the windows open,
in winter with the heater on.
They liked the side roads best: you sometimes found
Daughters of Norway smorgasbords in little Lutheran churches
or rustic places in remodeled old farmhouses
—the Spinning Wheel, the Weathervane, the White Turkey Inn—
or restaurants that still served family-style.

54

They'd have one drink before dinner,
lots of coffee after,
and always dessert.

Sometimes, if they happened to be in a small town,
they'd walk along Main Street and window-shop,
comparing prices there with prices in the city,
then they'd drive back home,
maybe this time by another road:
by the lake road, maybe, a pretty road
with the resort lights blinking
and shining on the water.

The Lord was good to them, they thought.
And this went on for many years
until they almost forgot
just what it was they used to do
before they'd found the Wishing Well,
the China Cupboard, and the Ship Ahoy.
This was their life now, they had time for themselves
to do what they wanted,
to do what they loved.

A JOURNEY BY RAILROAD

I was on an express with no stops scheduled. Yet the train slowed as it approached a platform, then braked to a halt. No one knew why.

At last, a voice came over the public address system: "This is the conductor speaking. The engineer has decided to stop here because this town has one of his favorite restaurants. He invites you to follow him for a real taste treat."

Laughing nervously, we spilled onto the platform and straggled up Main Street. Well, I had to admit, I do like a nice meal. Still, this is a pretty odd way to get to know a restaurant.

I also had to admit that the town wasn't much. In fact, it looked dumpy. We passed block after block of ramshackle houses with sagging porches and at last reached the restaurant. "Here we are, folks," the engineer shouted.

I can't say I felt heartened. The joint seemed hardly more than a saloon. Yet good meals can sometimes be had in unexpected places.

A shuffling waitress slapped down a gravy-stained menu. "Well," she said, "what'll it be?" Most of the items had already been scratched out, yet I managed to order. It took a long time for anything to arrive and, then, all the hot dishes were cold. But after looking around at my fellow passengers, I decided they were no better off than I was. Several were complaining about dirty forks. One had found a bug in the soup.

The engineer was sitting at the bar. Even though he was the guy who claimed he liked the food here, he was eating very little. But he was drinking quite a lot, and the way he teetered on his barstool made me suspect he was plastered, a suspicion confirmed when he fell unconscious to the floor, whereupon the bartender and the cook carried him off into the kitchen. And that was the last we saw of him.

What, we wondered, would happen now? The conductor got up, cleared his throat, and said, "I'm afraid we're stuck. The engineer, as you see, is indisposed. And because our train is still on the track, no other train can pass through. So, until our engineer regains his health and can move the train, I suggest we find accommodations at some hotel —"

"Ain't no hotels here," the waitress interjected. "No motels, neither."

"Then what I'd suggest," the conductor sighed, "is to go through the streets knocking on doors in search of hospitality." We did. But either no one responded or the doors were slammed when our needs were made known. And when I heard what sounded like a shotgun, I beat a hasty retreat.

We gathered, crestfallen, back at the restaurant. "Is there anyone here who knows how to drive a train?" the conductor asked in desperation. Of course, no one did.

Suddenly, he turned to me. "What about you? You look pretty smart." I blushed to hear it. "I bet you've even been to college." Which I couldn't deny. "So come on, drive this train for us." And before I could protest, he was dragging me back to the depot.

When we reached the engine he rummaged around and pulled out an engineer's cap, a blue chambray work shirt, and a pair of bib overalls. "Try these," he said. "It can get pretty greasy in there." I put them on. To my surprise, they fit rather well. I even fancied I cut a good figure in them. Maybe it won't be so bad, after all. It's actually nice and cozy here in the cab. And is there anyone who didn't want to drive a train as a kid?

Then the conductor — as good a soul as ever I've met — showed me where the whistle was. What a brave sound it makes. Listen! How lovely. And look: how the tracks shine up ahead!

Let's go.

THE PARADISE OF THE SHOPPING MALL

Every so often — but not so often
it aroused suspicion — he would fix his schedule
to make it appear he had lots of appointments
and leave for the rest of the afternoon.
But there were no appointments:
he'd just drive to a town a half-hour away.

When he got in his car
he'd feel this guilty pleasure —
as if he were hurrying toward a lover.
He tried to imagine what his friends would say
if he died on the road:
surely they'd wonder where he was going,
surely they'd think he was having an affair.
He also felt fear — a trespasser's fear —
that he might run into someone who knew him.
What would he say then?
How could he explain?

He was only going to a shopping mall;
that was all:
he went to this shopping mall —
the largest mall
in his part of the state.
He'd spend a few hours there
without anyone knowing it,
then turn around and drive home.

But when he was there, there in that mall,
there was so much. And it was always the same:
the same warmth in winter,
the same coolness in summer.
The music played, and little fountains played
in little gardens with little bushes and trees,
and you couldn't be sure if they were real or fake
no matter how long you paused to look.
The air would be pierced
by popcorn, chocolates, croissants, and fancy soaps
— outbursts of odors from the shops you passed —
and there would be stores with names
like Chess King, Cotton Ginny, and This End Up,

stores that sold jeans in a hundred different styles,
sporting goods stores with whole walls of sneakers,
and a gadget store with house fans, graters, and can openers
and battery powered flea collars for dogs.

Escalators would glide from the shopping floors to the food arcade
with its salad bars, taco stands, and China Delights,
and crystalline elevators adorned the walls
like stars in the heavens rising and setting.
Here was everything
in every season ever replenished.

And there were girls idling about, giggling,
or sitting on benches, gossiping, smoking.
There were cute housewives, too,
obviously glad they could spend a day shopping.
But he spoke to no one, did nothing.
Mostly, he looked;
he looked and he walked.

Yet sometimes he did buy something
as a secret reminder of where he had been,
what he had seen:
a shirt, perhaps, or a sweater,
something he could put on to summon up his adventure,
but something in a fashion not too outlandish,
so no one at home would think to inquire,
"I don't remember that.
Where did you buy it? How much did it cost?"

Then he'd stuff his package into his briefcase,
head for the parking lot,
and drive through the nightfall
back where he belonged,
the lights fading behind him
of the largest shopping mall
in his part of the state.

RAVING

Gerald died.
Dan read it in the paper:
a small item
about how he was found
dead in some flophouse.

They met in college.
Both were poets.
Both wrote free verse.
But Dan stayed on to teach
while Gerald took
job after job,
when he worked at all.

Dan got married.
Gerald was a drunk.
Dan used to wear a tie to class,
then things loosened up:
now he wears a turtleneck.
Gerald wore grimy chinos.
He was famous for raving.
He'd rave at readings
until they kicked him out.
Then he raved in bars,
and then in the street.

Neither wrote much.
Gerald was too busy raving.
Dan was busy
with his courses,
his family.
He loves teaching,
he loves his wife and kids,
yet somehow he regrets something,
he sometimes feels
his life lacks some dimension.

Now Gerald is dead,
dead in a flophouse.

Dan wonders
if he should start raving,
if he missed out by not raving,
if he should rave at least once,
just to have raved
at the edge of despair,
at the brink of the absurd.

He goes to a bar
down by the tracks
where nondescript men
watch a ballgame on television.
He has a few drinks.

The bar is a dump.
The ballgame is dull.
He has a headache already.
The men give him this funny look.
So he wonders
should he rave now.
But he doesn't know how.

He walks home,
mumbles something about drinking.
His wife gives him a funny look,
just like those men.

THE ROSENBERGS

They were very small.
Even smaller than that.
They meant well.
But they looked like Mickey and Minnie Mouse.

Wherever they went,
A spotlight hit them
And they had to dance.
So they tried to be gorgeous.
But when they moved, they moved funny.

And it keeps on like that.
Big people stand around
Looking down on them,
Not always the same people,
But always big, looking down
And pointing at them, saying,
"Hey, go on, dance!"
And, very small, they look like Mickey and Minnie Mouse dancing.
And they have to keep dancing
Until they don't know what they're doing.
But they try to look gorgeous
And never complain.

They keep having to do this again and again.
No matter what happens.
And, no matter what happens,
It always comes out wrong.

THE CONDEMNED

The photographs of condemned men
awaiting execution
stare from the papers.

Never before have they looked so beautiful.

No matter what their crimes may have been,
we love them now,
they make us embrace them.

In us is their afterlife.

SOCIAL STUDIES PROBLEMS

Gordon brought Rick, a street kid, up to his place. After some good sex and good dope, Rick asked if he could stay the night.

Q. What should Gordon have answered?

*

Gordon's old friend Donald had introduced him to Rick and Rick had often stayed overnight at Donald's. That very afternoon, because Donald was away on business, Gordon had let Rick into Donald's apartment with the spare set of keys he kept for it so Rick could pick up a jacket he'd left behind.

Finally, since Donald seemed to trust him, Gordon said Rick could stay, even though he didn't really know much about Rick.

Q. Is this what you would have done, had you been Gordon? Does it differ significantly from what you would have recommended Gordon to do?

*

During the night, Rick woke up with what he said was an asthma attack and told Gordon he had to go home for some medicine.

Q. Should Gordon have believed Rick?

*

After Rick had left, Gordon felt something fishy might be going on, so he looked around and discovered that his keys for Donald's apartment were missing.

Knowing that Donald would be gone until Monday, he rushed over there. The door was unlocked, the lights were on, Donald's stereo, tape deck, and television set had already been carted off, and there was a whole stack of stuff piled waiting for somebody to come by for a second load.

It was obvious who was responsible.

Q. Considering that Gordon has connections in the arts and Donald is important in high society and big business and both have been known to be generous to young men they like, does this mean that

a. *Rick was forced to do what he did by someone wielding power over him?*
b. *Rick desperately needed money in a hurry?*
c. *Rick had no artistic, social, or business ambitions, so he thought what the hell?*
d. *Rick was simply a stupid jerk?*

*

When Donald returned and learned what had happened, he cursed Gordon for having let Rick stay over; in fact, he nearly beat Gordon up.

Q. Was Donald's rage justified?

*

Then, having calmed down again, both Gordon and Donald agreed they ought to take steps.

Q. Should they press formal charges against Rick?

*

However, after a little investigation, they learned that Rick is still legally under age and therefore could, if he wished, press interesting counter-charges.

Q. Now what?

EUROPEAN LIONS: A DOZEN VIEWS

Six Views of Happy Lions

The eight lions that hold up this building
have stone rings in their mouths.
They bite at the stone as if it were bread.
It tastes good.

*

A lion on a fountain
just drools a bit.
He likes it.

*

Four lions poke their heads
from the base of a column
as if from a doghouse.
It is a lion house.
Each lion
has its own house.

*

This lion, up
on its hind legs, seems
to be hump-
ing a pillar
on which sits a crown
some-
thing like
the crown on
the lion's own head.
Power
is always such pleasure.

*

Children climb on the backs
of the two old lions
guarding the portal
and ride them like horses
on a merry-go-round.

The lions don't mind.
They may even be amused,
but they'd never deign to show it.

*

Four lions watch the four corners of a bishop.
Winged,
they could fly away if they wanted.
A cherub is inching toward each of the lions,
as if to pat its mane or smooth its feathers.
The lions are smiling, they're purring at the prospect.
They could fly away if they wanted, but they won't.

Six Views of Unhappy Lions

The lion sticking
out of the house wall
snarls day and night. Clearly,
the people who live there
mustn't like anyone
and the lion doesn't
even like them.

*

Every other beast
in this fountain spits
save for this lion.
Nor was he made to spit.
He was made to watch —
and, it turns out,
to get dirty.
Pigeons soil his head.
That's just not nice.

*

Four lions carry a thick stone slab.
Their faces are sad, they're the faces of old men.
They grit their teeth from the weight of their burden.
Their claws dig deep into the stone.
They suffer so much.

*

A knight is asleep
with a lion at his feet.

But one of his feet is jabbing the lion.
The lion's tongue hangs out.
He's fretful, he's gasping,
he'd like to scratch back.

*

In a panel on the door,
Daniel sits in the lions' den
with lions all around.
But the lions have been worn
by wind, rain, and time:
the lions can't assert themselves,
you can hardly tell they're lions,
they could almost be dogs.
And Daniel seems pretty feeble, too.

*

Long ago, someone thought,
"Here should be lions,"
then died without telling
anyone what he thought
and leaving the spot blank.
Ever since, the lions
have awaited their creation.
Since they'll wait forever,
they'll never die;
and yet they grieve,
for they'll never be.

Another View to Make It a Baker's Dozen

Here on this stone
the lion and the lamb
have lain down together:
the lamb
almost roaring with joy;
the lion, sheepish,
ready to bleat.
For some,
blessedness comes hard;
for others, it is second nature.

A Partial Index
to Myself

HERE YOU ARE WALKING
FORTY YEARS AGO

here you are
a little kid
walking to the store
because your grandpa has asked you
to buy him some chewing tobacco
and you know when you get there
they won't sell it to you
this has happened before
so you hope the street
will stretch on forever
and never arrive

for you're just a little kid
walking to the store
to buy grandpa his tobacco
which you know they won't sell you
though grandpa said
"Tell them who sent you"
you know that won't help
for this has happened before
and you'll have to come home
and give him his money back
and he'll say "You never told them
who sent you" though you did

but you know
they don't sell tobacco
to any little kids
so you hope the street
just keeps going
and never gets there
where you'll have to say
"Art sent me
Art from Taylor St.
he's my grandpa
he wants his chewing tobacco"
and they'll say
as they have to
"But we can't sell tobacco
to any little kids
no matter who their grandpas are

now run along
and be sure you tell Art that"

yet here you are again
and you feel so helpless
you want to cry
for you'll have to ask for the tobacco
grandpa keeps asking you to buy him
the tobacco you can't buy
no matter how much money you have
and will have to give back
while your grandpa says "You never said
it was for Art
Art from Taylor St."
though you did say it you did
you said "It's not for me I'm here for Art
it's all for Art"
and they said "Kid
we can't do that for Art
why don't you tell Art that?"
which you do but still he says
"I bet you never said who sent you
if they knew Art sent you
they'd sell you the tobacco" but they won't
and here you are knowing
what you'll say
what they'll say
what grandpa will say back home
and you're walking to the store
on a street you hope
will never ever get there
but it will you know it has to
for this has happened before
and will again
just like this
even when you're old
you know you'll still
have to hear yourself say
"Art sent me it's for Art"
you know that's how it will be
always
though you're just a little kid

BLUES ON THE RANCH

We spend our evenings on the ranch
listening to our denims fade,
hearing the throb of blue threads turning white
and the soft twangings as the knees wear away.

You can't see them change, it's like watching a clock:
you look and you look and nothing has happened,
then, after you do something, when you look again
there's a place worn right through and another one starting.

But in the evening when the sun goes down
the denim starts chanting of its day of hard labor
while the rivets tap like little castanets—
O hear your jeans singing, drunk on your sweat.

They know nothing but you, they hug you, their hero.
O hear your jeans fading as they live out your life.

A POEM OF COFFEE

Sometimes, even as you drink it, you cannot say how it tastes. Yet you keep on drinking it, day and night.

It is the winter morning with the snow still falling. The summer morning with the light on the curtains. It is the hot summer night in the greasy spoon, the cold winter night there because the car won't start, when you sit for hours with nothing to do, so you lift your cup slowly to have something to do. It is the lead in pencils, the ink in pens. It is riding the el past kitchen windows. It is a porchlight left on. A light left on at the back of the house.

It is a snowy morning in winter, a summer light on the curtains. It is the drive across Ohio. The drive across Texas. Trucks shifting gears. The way a Greyhound bus smells. It is listening to the men with murmuring voices who play records on FM all through the night. It is driving at night with the car radio booming. It is long talks with mother. Chainsmoking cigarettes. And an ashtray filled with cigarette stubs. A press room. A seminar room. A county jail in the sticks. It is waiting to change buses. Waiting to change trains in dim, empty stations. It is staying up late. Or getting up early. It is the first thing after toothpaste. The last thing before bed.

It is the winter morning with the snow still falling, the summer morning with the light on the curtains. It is a habit. A ritual. Your job. Your small pleasure. It is what keeps you going day after day, what makes you get by on your nerves alone. It is what you take in with the Sunday paper. It is printing, a black typeface. And a piece of white paper without any words. It is darkness in the pencil, snow on the page.

It is this piece of white paper with this snow still falling, this light on the curtains, this pencil writing. It is these words before you, any time of the year, any time, any day.

PASSING

Passing on the bus
you look to see
who's entering the gay bar

and who else on the bus
has looked to see
who's going to the bar

and who on the bus
is looking to see
who looks at that bar

THE DRAMA

*Scene: The auditorium of a theatre. Two seated theatre-goers
are discovered staring at the stage.*

First Theatregoer (*after a pause*): I can't understand this play. I don't like it.

Second: But it hasn't started yet. So how do you know you can't understand it?

First: I can tell I don't like this play, and I don't like things I can't understand.

(*Short pause*)

Second: But it still hasn't started. Shouldn't it have started, though? Oughtn't it to start soon?

First: What good would that do? I don't understand it.

Second: Maybe it *has* started. Maybe it started while we were talking. Maybe it's going on right now. Maybe we should be quiet and pay attention.

(*Long pause*)

First: I don't understand this play.

Second: But nothing seems to be happening.

First: I don't understand it.

Second: Maybe it's really intermission now. Maybe we should go out and drink orangeade.

(*They rise, exit, and drink orangeade in the lobby. Then they return and sit down.*)

First: I don't understand this play. I don't like it.

Second: But nothing's happened yet. Why doesn't something happen? Will anything ever happen?

First: Now, now, just be patient. I don't understand it, either, but see how patient I am.

Second: Patient? *You*, patient? You've done nothing but whine ever since we got here!

First: Whine? What do you mean, *whine*? All I've done is give you an honest opinion: what's wrong with giving an honest opinion about a play?

Second: But nothing's happened!

First: I just don't understand it.

Second: What I think is, we've missed the play. I had to pay so much attention to you and your whining that I had no time for the play. And now it's over and we've missed it.

First: I didn't like it.

Second: So what do we do now? Since it was entirely your fault that we missed the play, we can't very well ask for our money back. We've wasted a whole evening.

First: I didn't like it, not one bit of it!

Second: I suppose all we can do now is go. Let's go.

First: I still don't understand this play. I bet it gets terrible reviews.

(*They exit.*)

THE POET WHO ALMOST RAN OVER
CARL SANDBURG

There once was a poet
who almost ran over Carl Sandburg.
This was back when
the poet was young
and Carl Sandburg was old.

One time, old Carl Sandburg was visiting
the college where this young poet taught
and, out of politeness,
the poet and his wife
invited Carl Sandburg
up to their home,
even though the poet didn't like
Carl Sandburg's poetry
and Carl Sandburg had never even heard of this poet.

Yet Carl Sandburg came
and they sat around talking.
Carl Sandburg did the talking,
and he did some more talking,
and then it was time
for Carl Sandburg to leave.

The poet offered to give him a lift.
"Wait here, I'll bring the car around,"
the poet said, and he started to back
his car down the driveway
when he looked around and—damn!—
there was Carl Sandburg
standing right
in the way of his car,
gazing at the moon.

A few seconds more
and the poet would have done it:
he'd have run over Carl Sandburg,
squashed him flat as a pancake,
except the poet
slammed on his brakes
and the car stopped short

only a few inches from where Carl Sandburg still stood
gazing up at the moon.

The poet broke out
into a cold, cold sweat.

"I almost ran over
Carl Sandburg just now.
Good God!" he thought,
"what that would have done
to the rest of my career!
No matter where I went,
no matter what I wrote,
I'd be known as the poet
who ran over Carl Sandburg
and no one would ever
take me seriously again
or dare to publish any of my poems —
and all because
I ran over Carl Sandburg!

"But I didn't
run over Carl Sandburg," he realized.
"The old goat is opening
the door of my car.
I'm not the poet who ran over Carl Sandburg,
I'm the poet who almost
ran over Carl Sandburg."
And, suddenly, it struck him
his career was made.

From that day on
he told this story
at every literary cocktail party,
poetry reading, or conference he went to.
He would laugh at himself,
and the people who heard him would smile and laugh back,
and then, out of curiosity,
they'd buy his books,
simply because they knew who he was:
he was the young poet
who'd almost run over old Carl Sandburg
way back when.

THIS TIME BETWEEN US

Now, after all this time, we've met. We sit across from each other and smile.

What do we want of each other? What do we need?

I look at you and think, "Young, yes. But, fortunately, not a child. Not a mere child."

I think again: "And I'm not so old. Not all that old. I still seem young enough, I think."

You ask if I remember something. Yes, of course. Of course you don't. You can't. You're young.

So I say how it was. Then you tell me something I didn't know. We're talking now. Thank God, we're talking.

If you were younger or I were older by only a few years, what stammerings there might be, what bowings and scrapings in deference, what posturings of authority. Yet if we were both the same age, what point would there be in meeting, both of us knowing and saying the same things?

We are lucky. We can talk. You want to know what I remember about something. I need to hear you say what you think.

We sit close together with this time between us. It is just the right time. No wonder we smile. Next time we meet, we shall both say, I feel sure of it, "What's new?"

MURDERS

As I look down from the headline
to the account of the next new violent death,
I tremble to read the life of the accused —
and am relieved

to find he has a jealous wife,
a mistress, or a dream girl
he's never met but wants to impress.

I know then I won't be held as an accomplice.
I can go free.

Someday, though
— and it's bound to happen someday —
the accused will be
unambiguously gay.

Then we may all be charged and found guilty.

*

There are these other cases, too:
little items buried away
about bachelors stabbed
in their messed-up apartments
or a Central Park bush.

Their stories just come and go through the papers:
it's often hard to find out
who the suspects are
or when their trials come up.
No one seems to care.

*

Some nights I wonder
what sort of home life
any person I'd bring home
who'd stab me would have,
how discreetly reporters
would handle my story
and what the defense
and the verdict would be.

THE PARTICULARS

Consider the particulars.

*

The god of the toothpaste is not the god of the davenport.
The god of my knees is not the god of last Tuesday.
The god of the motorcar is not the god of pajamas.
The god of stuttering is not the god of disinfectant.
The god of the ledger is not the god of the wine bottle.
And so on in this vein.
Each thing with its own god.

*

Consider, there were so many things.   Each claimed attention.
The early morning was hazy.   We could hardly see the trees.
I had cried out in the night.   You calmed me, as always.
It was the old shudders come back.   I've learned to outlive them.
After that, I slept soundly.   I got up and packed.
The mist was rising.   There were patches of sun.
We could see the fields clearly.   But the hills were still dim.
A man was out walking.   He met another man with a dog.
There was a low mound like a ruin.   They kept walking toward it.
We left them behind.   Our train crossed a bridge.
Someone came by selling coffee.   It was tasteless, but hot.
There were more houses now.   And schools, hospitals, factories.
And here was our station.   Bells rang in the distance.
We saw posters for the opera.   We saw posters for bars.
My suitcase felt heavy.   We wondered about taxis.
We wondered about restaurants.   Were we wise to have come?
It was now mid-October.   We walked through fallen leaves.
We approached what was next.   And, next, things would happen.

*

Consider the particulars,

Those forces working,

Each with its god.

A WAY OF HAPPENING

...poetry makes nothing happen
—W.H. Auden

But at least
we can try to make
poetry
make something happen.

Therefore
I shall not conceal
anything
in this poem,

and if the names in it
are slightly changed,
that's to prevent
needless embarrassment:
but anyone involved
will recognize himself instantly,
that I guarantee.

This, then,
is a calling out,
an incitement to action.

In college
my roommate
was Robert Breuer,
who one year was elected
dorm president,
he was that nice,
good-looking,
and sharp.

Across the hall
lived Nick Clark,
tall, scrawny,
built like a stork,
a ferocious brain
and High Church choir singer

who developed a crush
on Bob Breuer.

And when Bob
found out
he shunned him
totally,
wouldn't even
say hello to him,

and since such things
seemed strange to us,
the rest of us shunned him, too.

We were seniors when it happened.
Graduation
solved everthing:
we all went away
(and thank goodness,
for by then
I'd developed a crush
on Ken Blakeslee,
but never mind
about that).

Now
I want to try
to make something happen.
Does anyone know
whatever became of anyone
I've mentioned in this poem?
If so,
please contact me
in care of this publication.

Or, perhaps, this is not
the right publication
for such a message to appear in.
Then let me know and tell me
what publication you think is.

THE WINDOW IN LOVE

A window saw something that it loved go by.

*

The window waited for it to go by again.

*

Later that day or the next day or the next
What the window loved went by once more.

*

The window was happy.

*

The window kept looking
At everything out there
But the window was looking
Only for what it loved.

*

Day after day night after night
The window waited for what it loved to go by.

*

Then the window felt sad when what it loved was gone.

*

Then the window grew scared
That what it loved was gone forever.

*

So the window consoled itself
By turning everything out there into the image of what it loved.

*

That taxi in the street that woman with the dog
That cloud in the sky that cloudless sky that leaf that barren bough

That snow that rain that garbage can those kids
That brick wall opposite that window in that wall.

    *

All that the window saw now was an image of what it loved.

    *

All the window saw now was so much what it loved
The window forgot what the first thing it loved was like.

    *

Day after day night after night
The window gleamed in its wall and everything out there gleamed back
And whatever went by was what the window loved most.

PERFECTION

Late Saturday nights
after the dinner and the play or the movie
and after the first Sunday papers have come out

those late Saturday nights
when it's raining in spring or snowing in winter
and almost no cars pass by any more

on those late Saturday nights
nothing needs to be done
but the Sunday crossword

which never gets done
for its paths stretch on
deeper and deeper into the night

as word after word falls into place
but never the last word
and the mind rejoices

at how the right words can fill
this noble emptiness
and yet lead to more words

then the lamp stays lit
the night stays dark
and as long as the puzzle lasts is perfection

surely jails and asylums have opened their doors
surely no one lacks riches there is no one cast down
no one frets sleepless or cries in his dreams

war and cancer can never return
there is nothing but words and the meanings of words
and I look up from the puzzle and tell you "I love you"

A PARTIAL INDEX TO MYSELF

A   aardvarks
       aberrations
       aftershave
       architecture
       artifice

B   Bach
       ballet
       bark worse than a bite
       bed
       befuddlement
       birthdays

C   caves
       champagne
       chocolate cake
       Christmas
       coffee
       contradictions
       cowboys
       crosswords

D   darkness
       death
       decadence
       denim
       dental floss
       deodorant
       dilettantism
       disguises

E   enigmas
       erections

F   fate
       fetishes
       foolishness

G   gay
       ghosts
       gibberish
       gnomes
       gnus fit to print
       grins

H   haircuts
       happenstance
       hide-and-seek
       higgledy-piggledy
       huggermugger
       hypochondria

I   ice cream
       imagination
       infatuation
       ink
       interior decoration
       interior monologue
       -isms
       it

J   jackanapes
       jackass
       jack-in-the-box
       jack rabbit

K   keys
       kinks
       kisses

L   labyrinths
       laziness
       leather
       Liebeslieder Walzer
       lions
       llamas

M	manicure scissors	S	safari outfitting
	maps		safety valves
	menus		secrets
	mice		sedition
	money		seduction
	myopia		shaggy dogs and their stories
			shudders
N	nail picking		smorgasbord
	nit picking		
	nuts	T	time
			time and tide
O	okay		
		U	universal joints
P	pandas	V	vacations
	pandemonium		vexations
	paradox		vices
	parties		volcanos
	peace marches		
	pecan pie	W	warts
	penguins		weight watching
	piano lessons		wiggles
	pizza		wine
	poetry		
	poodles	X	X-ray eyes
	pussycats		
		Y	yellow journalism
Q	quackery		Yellow Pages
	queasiness		Yellowstone National Park
	questions		you and the night and the music
R	rain	Z	zeppelins
	rasps		zero hour
	remnants		zippers
	revenants		zoos
	rhythm		
	romanticism		
	Rosetta stone		
	rubbish